First World War
and Army of Occupation
War Diary
France, Belgium and Germany

59 DIVISION
178 Infantry Brigade
Sherwood Foresters
(Nottinghamshire and Derbyshire Regiment)
2/6th Battalion
25 February 1917 - 31 July 1918

WO95/3025/3

The Naval & Military Press Ltd
www.nmarchive.com
Published in association with The National Archives

Published by

The Naval & Military Press Ltd

Unit 10 Ridgewood Industrial Park,

Uckfield, East Sussex,

TN22 5QE England

Tel: +44 (0) 1825 749494

www.naval-military-press.com

www.nmarchive.com

This diary has been reprinted in facsimile from the original. Any imperfections are inevitably reproduced and the quality may fall short of modern type and cartographic standards.

© Crown Copyright
Images reproduced by permission of The National Archives, London, England, 2015.

Contents

Document type	Place/Title	Date From	Date To
Heading	WO 3025 59th Div 178 Infy Bde 2-6th Bn Notts & derby Regt 1917 Feb-1918 July		
Heading	59th Division 178th Infy Bde 2-6th BN Notts & Derby Regt Feb 1917-July 1918		
Heading	War Diary Of 2/6th Bn The Sherwood Foresters From 25th February 1917 To 28th February 1917		
War Diary	No 6 Camp Hurdcott	25/02/1917	25/02/1917
War Diary	Fovant	26/02/1917	26/02/1917
War Diary	Boulogne	28/02/1917	28/02/1917
Miscellaneous	Drill Hall Newark-On-Trent Feb 13th 1928		
Miscellaneous	Lieut-Colonel A.C Clarke T.D Drill Hall Newark-On-Trent		
Heading	2/6th Bn The Sherwood Foresters (notts And Derby Regiment) War Diary For Month Of March 1917		
War Diary	Pontde Metz	01/03/1917	01/03/1917
War Diary	Glisy	02/03/1917	02/03/1917
War Diary	Warfusee	02/03/1917	09/03/1917
War Diary	Foucaucourt	09/03/1917	16/03/1917
War Diary	Berny	16/03/1917	19/03/1917
War Diary	Cizancourt	20/03/1917	22/03/1917
War Diary	P C Nancy	26/03/1917	26/03/1917
War Diary	Brie	27/03/1917	27/03/1917
War Diary	Vraignes	28/03/1917	29/03/1917
Heading	2/6th Bn The Sherwood Foresters (notts And Derby Regiment) War Diary For Month Of April 1917		
War Diary	Vraignes	31/03/1917	31/03/1917
War Diary	Bernes	31/03/1917	31/03/1917
War Diary	Vendelles	01/04/1917	01/04/1917
War Diary	Bernes	03/04/1917	06/04/1917
War Diary	Hancourt	07/04/1917	19/04/1917
War Diary	Roisel	22/04/1917	29/04/1917
Heading	2/6th Bn Sherwood Foresters Notts & Derby Regiment War Diary For Month Of May 1917		
War Diary	Roisel	01/05/1917	01/05/1917
War Diary	L 10 C 4.3	02/05/1917	06/05/1917
War Diary	Hancourt	09/05/1917	19/05/1917
War Diary	Villers Faucon	21/05/1917	21/05/1917
War Diary	Saulcourt	23/05/1917	30/05/1917
Heading	2/6th Bn The Sherwood Foresters War Diary for Month Of June 1917		
War Diary	Equancourt	01/06/1917	01/06/1917
War Diary	Metz	05/06/1917	11/06/1917
War Diary	Equancourt	11/06/1917	21/06/1917
War Diary	Beaucamp	21/06/1917	30/06/1917
Heading	War Diary 2/6th Bn The Sherwood Foresters July 1917		
War Diary	Q.18.b.88 Ref 57c SE	01/07/1917	08/07/1917
War Diary	Dessart Wood	08/07/1917	08/07/1917
War Diary	O.35d.7.7	10/07/1917	31/07/1917
Heading	2nd/6th Bn Sherwood Foresters War Diary August 1917		

War Diary	Le Mesnil O35 Central 57c SW	01/08/1917	31/08/1917
Heading	2/6th Bn Sherwood Foresters War Diary September 1917		
War Diary	Winnezeele J.2b.8.8 (Sheet 27)	01/09/1917	19/09/1917
War Diary	Forge L.7d.b.3 (Sheet 27)	20/09/1917	22/09/1917
War Diary	Vlamertinghe H.11.b.8.3 (Sheet 28)	23/09/1917	30/09/1917
Heading	War Diary 2/6th Bn The Sherwood Foresters October 1917		
War Diary	Wieltje	01/10/1917	01/10/1917
War Diary	Vlamertinghe	02/10/1917	02/10/1917
War Diary	Boesegham	03/10/1917	05/10/1917
War Diary	Coyecque	06/10/1917	10/10/1917
War Diary	Fiefs	11/10/1917	11/10/1917
War Diary	Tangry	12/10/1917	12/10/1917
War Diary	Barlin	13/10/1917	13/10/1917
War Diary	Gody-Servins	14/10/1917	21/10/1917
War Diary	Avion	22/10/1917	31/10/1917
Heading	War Diary 2/6th Bn Sherwood Foresters November 1917		
War Diary	Avion	01/11/1917	06/11/1917
War Diary	Carency	07/11/1917	13/11/1917
War Diary	Duisans	14/11/1917	18/11/1917
War Diary	Hendecourt	19/11/1917	19/11/1917
War Diary	Gomiecourt	21/11/1917	25/11/1917
War Diary	Queens Cross	25/11/1917	30/11/1917
Miscellaneous	Operations Of 2/6th Sherwood Foresters		
Heading	War Diary For Dec 1917 2/6th Bn Sherwood Foresters		
War Diary	La Vacquerie R 16 (special Sheet 57c NE SE And 57b NW SW)	01/12/1917	03/12/1917
War Diary	Trescault	05/12/1917	08/12/1917
War Diary	Flesquires	09/12/1917	17/12/1917
War Diary	Bertincourt	18/12/1917	20/12/1917
War Diary	Rocquigny	21/12/1917	21/12/1917
War Diary	Beaulencourt	22/12/1917	25/12/1917
War Diary	Magnicourt	26/12/1917	31/12/1917
Heading	2/6th Battalion Sherwood Foresters War Diary January 1918		
War Diary	Magnicourt Sur-Canch H.10.d (Sheet 51c)	01/01/1918	30/01/1918
Heading	2/6 Bn The Sherwood Foresters War Diary February 1918		
War Diary	Magnicourt Sur-Canch H.10.d. (Sheet 51c)	01/02/1918	04/02/1918
War Diary	H.4.d	05/02/1918	07/02/1918
War Diary	Gouy-En-Artois Q.13.c (51c)	08/02/1918	08/02/1918
War Diary	Durham Camp S.11.a (51c)	09/02/1918	09/02/1918
War Diary	Mory L'abbaye B.22.a (57c)	10/02/1918	11/02/1918
War Diary	B.21.d (Sheet 57c N.W)	23/02/1918	25/02/1918
War Diary	Sheet 51b S.W.	26/02/1918	28/02/1918
Heading	59th Division 178th Infantry Brigade 2/6th Battalion Sherwood Forester March 1918		
Miscellaneous	HQrs 59th Division	28/04/1918	28/04/1918
Heading	2/6th Bn The Sherwood Foresters War Diary March 1918		
War Diary	Sheet 57b U.25b.3.4	01/03/1918	02/03/1918
War Diary	North Camp Mory B.21b.8.7	02/03/1918	10/03/1918
War Diary	U.14	11/03/1918	21/03/1918
War Diary	Ayette	22/03/1918	23/03/1918

War Diary	Senlis	24/03/1918	24/03/1918
War Diary	Esbler	25/03/1918	25/03/1918
War Diary	Fieffes	26/03/1918	26/03/1918
War Diary	Cambligneul	28/03/1918	30/03/1918
Miscellaneous	Narrative Of The German Attack Against The 2/6th Battalion Sherwood Forester		
Miscellaneous	Copy Of Letters From Major AC Clarks		
Diagram etc	Ecoust (Neighbourhood) From Memory		
Miscellaneous	Narrative Of The German Attack Against The 2/6th Battalion Sherwood Foresters		
Heading	178th Brigade 59th Division 2/6th Battalion Notts & Derby Regiment April 1918		
Heading	War Diary 2/6th Bn The Sherwood Foresters April 1918		
War Diary	Cambligneul	01/04/1918	07/04/1918
War Diary	Winnezeele	08/04/1918	10/04/1918
War Diary	Brandhoek	11/04/1918	21/04/1918
War Diary	Houtkerque	26/04/1918	26/04/1918
War Diary	F.25.b.1.4	27/04/1918	28/04/1918
War Diary	Houtkerque	29/04/1918	30/04/1918
Miscellaneous	Warning Order 71st Infantry Brigade	31/07/1918	31/07/1918
Miscellaneous	71st Infantry Brigade Warning Order Issued	31/07/1918	31/07/1918
Heading	War Diary 2/6 Bn The Sherwood Foresters May 1918		
War Diary	Houtkerque E20.b.25.75 K17.a.3.3	01/05/1918	05/05/1918
War Diary	Hazebrouck 5a St Omer	06/05/1918	07/05/1918
War Diary	Blessy 5d.95.40	09/05/1918	09/05/1918
War Diary	Sheet 36b Bours H34.b.9.7	10/05/1918	31/05/1918
Heading	War Diary Of HQ 2/6 Sherwood Foresters (Training Cadre) For June 1918		
Heading	War Diary 2/6th Bn The Sherwood Foresters June 1918		
Miscellaneous	Headquarters 178th Infantry Brigade	01/07/1918	01/07/1918
War Diary	Bours H.34.b.9.7 (44 B)	01/06/1918	17/06/1918
War Diary	Fontaine-Lez-Boulane F.29.d.8.8 (44c Eastern Half)	18/06/1918	30/06/1918
Heading	2/6th Bn The Sherwood Foresters War Diary July 1918		
War Diary	Fontaine Lez Boulans	01/07/1918	09/07/1918
War Diary	F.29.d.8.8 Sheet 44c Eastern Half	23/07/1918	23/07/1918
War Diary	Barly P15a.a.8 Sheet 51.C	28/07/1918	31/07/1918

WO 3025
59 Div 178 INFY Bde

2-6th Bn Notts + Derby Regt

1917 Feb — 1918 July

59TH DIVISION
178TH INFY BDE

2-6TH BN NOTTS & DERBY REGT
FEB 1917- JLY 1918

DISBANDED

CONFIDENTIAL 1st/39 Vol 1

WAR DIARY
of
2/6th Bn. The Sherwood Foresters.

from 25th February 1917 ---- to 28th February 1917.

(Volume 1)

Army Form C. 2118.

WAR DIARY
6th Bn. Sherwood Foresters,
or
INTELLIGENCE SUMMARY.

(Erase heading not required.)

For period 25th to 28th Feb 1917

Hour, Date, Place	Summary of Events and Information	Remarks and references to Appendices
25/2/17 No 6 Camp HURDCOTT	Bn. marches out of Camp.	J.M.
26/2/17 FOVANT	Bn. entrains and proceeds to FOLKESTONE. Crosses from FOLKESTONE to BOULOGNE. Spends night 26/27 Feb: in St MARTIN Camp.	J.M.
28/2/17 BOULOGNE	Bn. entrains at BOULOGNE and proceeds to SALEUX (près d'AMIENS) detraining there and marching to PONT DE METZ, where transport rejoins Bn. Night spent in Billets.	J.M.

H.S. Hodgkin Lt. Col
Comm'dg 2/6 Sherwood Foresters
7-3-17.

Drill Hall
Newark-on-Trent.

Feb. 13th. 1928.

Historical Section (Military Branch)
  Committee of Imperial Defence
      Audit House
          Victoria Embankment, E.C.4.

   With reference to your letter 1918/D, dated Dec. 30th. 1927, I enclose herewith the notes I made of the part played by 2/6 Battn. The Sherwood Foresters, in the Battle of Cambrai 1917.

This account has already been filed with the records of the Battn., consequently there is no need for you to forward it, after you have made what use you may wish to do of it.

A.C.Clarke

Lt. Col.
Commdg. 8th. Sherwood Foresters.

Ref: CAM/1917.   15th February 1928

Lieut.-Colonel A.C.Clarke T.D.
    Drill Hall
        Newark-on-Trent.

    We are extremely obliged for your letter of 13th February, and for the account of the part played by the 2/6th Battn. The Sherwood Foresters in the Battle of Cambrai, 1917, which we have placed with the war diary.

                                                                        for
Director, Historical Section, Military Branch.

WAR DIARY
or
INTELLIGENCE SUMMARY

(Erase heading not required.)

Army Form C. 2118.

Vol II

CONFIDENTIAL

2/6TH BN. THE SHERWOOD FORESTERS
(NOTTS. AND DERBY REGIMENT)

WAR DIARY
FOR
MONTH OF MARCH 1917

WAR DIARY or INTELLIGENCE SUMMARY

2/6 Bn. The Sherwood Foresters,
Notts & Derby Regt.

Army Form C. 2118

(Erase heading not required.)

Instructions regarding War Diaries and Intelligence Summaries are contained in F.S. Regs., Part II. and the Staff Manual respectively. Title Pages will be prepared in manuscript.

Place	Date	Hour	Summary of Events and Information.	Remarks and references to Appendices
PONT DE METZ	1/3/17	9.30am	Bn. marches via AMIENS to GLISY. night spent in billets	J.P.W.
GLISY.	2/3/17	8.30am	Bn. marches via VILLERS-BRETONNEAUX to WARFUSEE - ABANCOURT.	J.P.W.
WARFUSEE.	2/3/17 to 9/3/17		Bn. in billets.	J.P.W.
"	9/3/17	12.30pm	Bn. marched to FOUCAUCOURT.	J.P.W.
FOUCAUCOURT	9/3/17 to 15/3/17		Bn. in Billets.	J.P.W.
"	15/3/17		4 Platoons attached for instruction to 5th Bn. Leicester Regt.	J.P.W.
"	16/3/17	7.15pm	Bn. marches to BERNY. N.32.d.8.2 (Map Sheet 62°SW.) & is attached to 176th Inf. Bde., and takes up position in reserve line.	J.P.W.
BERNY.	17/3/17 to 19/3/17		In reserve line at BERNY.	J.P.W.
"	19/3/17	9.0am	Bn. marches to CIZANCOURT via MAZANCOURT and MISERY.	J.P.W.
"	"	3.0pm	Two companies cross River SOMME & take up positions in Notre Dame Trench (Mapsheet 62°SW) U.16.c.4.9 to U.16.a.8.9. and Sardinelle Alley. U.15.d.2.35 U.16.c.4.9.	J.P.W.
CIZANCOURT	20/3/17	6.0pm	One company moves to outpost position in FOURQUES as support to Cavalry.	J.P.W.
"	22/3/17	9.0am	Outpost Coy withdrawn. Bn. marches via VILLERS-CARBONNEL to P.C. NANCY on ESTREES-VILLERS-CARBONNEL Road.	J.P.W.
P.C. NANCY	26/3/17	1.0pm	Bn. marches to BRIE and occupies bridgehead defences. Bn. H.Q. at O.28.c.9.5.2.5 (Map Sheet 62°S.W.)	J.P.W.
BRIE.	27/3/17	2.0pm	Bn. marches to VRAIGNES. Bn. H.Q. at Q.19.B.7.3.15 (Map Sheet 62°S.E.)	J.P.W.
VRAIGNES.	28/3/17	7.0pm	Two Coys take up outpost position & dig in on line covering Q.4.A.8.1. K.33.d.5.1. Q.22.b.9.9.	J.P.W.
"	29/3/17	7.0pm	Two Coys out digging trench in support on line to Pots at Q.22.B.9.9. and Q.17.c.4.5.	J.P.W.

H. Jeff
Lt.Col.
Comdg. 2/6 The Sherwood Foresters

Army Form C. 2118.

WAR DIARY
or
INTELLIGENCE SUMMARY
(Erase heading not required.)

59/175 ORIGINAL. Vol 3.

S.W.

2/6TH BN THE SHERWOOD FORESTERS.
(NOTTS. AND DERBY REGIMENT.)

―― WAR DIARY. ――

FOR

MONTH OF APRIL, 1917.

WAR DIARY or INTELLIGENCE SUMMARY

Army Form C. 2118

ORIGINAL

Place	Date	Hour	Summary of Events and Information	Remarks and references to Appendices
VRAIGNES BERNES	31-3-17	2 am	Batta left for BERNES & reached enemy Q.4.a.4.2.	10 afb
BERNES	31-3-17	2.0 pm	Batta launched attack from red & Q. & Lehmann attacked in wave under heavy hostile shell fire. Wood carried. Village successfully outflanked and captured. JEANCOURT 10 km enemy captured. Batta then took up position from R.6.55 to R.10.25.	
VENDELLES	1-4-17	11.30 am	Two Coys with Battn were relieved & withdrew by BERNES. Remaining two coys went in support to 25th which was forward Battn at BERNES at km stretch R.14.2.5A Red 9.1. Red aimed Battn at BERNES at 12 noon 2-4-17	10 afb
BERNES	3-4-17	7 am	2nd Bn B Coy went in support of 25 afterward forward Battn to VENDELLES returning at 11.0 am same am.	28 afb
BERNES	4-4-17	9-4 pm	2nd D Coy went to VENDELLES & dug holes along line from L.27 & 2.2 to L.33.L.2.1. Returning 1.0 am 5.5.17	10 afb
BERNES	6-4-17	9.0 am	Batta mounted to R.9.0.4.5 in support of 2/5 Linc at ???	10 afb
HANCOURT	7-4-17	3.30 am	2/5 attacked enemy position SE of LE VERGUIER. Batt withdrawn to HANCOURT	10 afb
HANCOURT	16-4-17	2.30 pm	Inspection of Battn by Hon Gen'l B J Power DB LHC bringing Sqr of Cav in Co of 17 9th Bde according to Myala any Syr in Co R G 6/th Linc Regt	10 afb
HANCOURT	17-4-17	12.30 pm	Fys Red 3rd Sinnafatt & Sol Duchy 17 9th Bde according Myala Syr in Co	20 afb
HANCOURT	19-4-17	2.0 pm	Batta marched to L.38.78 and took over the front line from 2/5th Lincolnshire Regt.	20 afb
POISEL	22-4-17	9.0 am	Batta was relieved by 2/7 Ch Bn and marched back to POISEL in reserve	2 afb

1875 Wt. W593/826 1,000,000 4/15 J.B.C. & A. A.D.S.S./Forms/C.2118.

WAR DIARY
or
INTELLIGENCE SUMMARY

Army Form C. 2118

Place	Date	Hour	Summary of Events and Information	Remarks and references to Appendices
ROISEL	29.9.18	1am	Battn marched to HARGICOURT ROAD from L.11.b.05 to L.11.b.5.0 to L.11.b.5.0.15 deploy prior to an attack on QUARRIES and COLOGNE FARM (L.6.c. & 6). The attack was launched at 3.55 am and the QUARRIES were successfully captured and a line was consolidated EAST of the QUARRIES from L.5.d.9.5 to L.11.b.9.9. Seven prisoners and 1 trench mortar were captured by 2/7th.	[appendix] [appendix] [appendix]
ROISEL	29.9.18	2pm	Battn marched to Roisel having been relieved by 2/7th Sherwood Foresters.	

H.L. Hodgkin
Lieut. Col.
Comdg. 2/6th Bn the Sherwood Foresters.

Army Form C. 2118.

WAR DIARY
or
INTELLIGENCE SUMMARY
(Erase heading not required.)

2/6th. Bn. Sherwood Foresters.

Notts & Derby Regiment.

War Diary

for

Month of May 1917.

H.W.

57/178

Vol 4

Instructions regarding War Diaries and Intelligence Summaries are contained in F. S. Regs., Part II. and the Staff Manual respectively. Title Pages will be prepared in manuscript.

WAR DIARY
or
INTELLIGENCE SUMMARY
(*Erase heading not required.*)

Army Form C. 2118

Place	Date	Hour	Summary of Events and Information	Remarks and references to Appendices
ROISEL	1/5/17		Fighting Strength Offrs 14 O Ranks 392	
		8 pm	Battalion moved into the line to relieve 2/5th Sherwood Foresters Hdqrs at L10 c 4 3 (Ref 62 c NE). The 2/4th Lincolnshire Regt were on our right and the 2/5th Sher. Foresters on our left	W.H.B.
L 10 c 4 3.	2nd to 6/5/17		No incidents of any importance occurred during this tour. Casualties one Other Rank slightly wounded	
	6/5/17	11.45 pm	Battalion relieved by 2/5th North Staffordshire Regt and marched into Divisional Reserve at HANCOURT	W.H.B.
HANCOURT	9/5/17	2.30 pm	Lt Genl Sir W P Pulteney KCB, KCMG, DSO [illegible] III Corps Commander presented to the following officers & men their awards for gallantry & devotion to duty during the action in [illegible] Capt [illegible] Langford — Military Cross 2Lt [illegible] Bradley do do [illegible] Military Medal [illegible] do do The Corps Comdr expressed his appreciation of the smart appearance of the Battalion.	W.H.B.

1875 Wt. W593/826 1,000,000 4/15 J.B.C. & A. A.D.S.S./Forms/C. 2118.

Army Form C. 2118

WAR DIARY
or
INTELLIGENCE SUMMARY
(Erase heading not required.)

Place	Date	Hour	Summary of Events and Information	Remarks and references to Appendices
HANCOURT	11/5		Capt Meadows Ernest Kellner [illegible] awarded the Military Cross for gallantry [illegible] at VENDORT on 3rd March 1917	B/M.G
	13/5	11am	The Commanding Officer (on behalf of the D. enemy Lewis awarded MERITORIOUS SERVICE CARDS to the following L.G.D [illegible] of the Battalion —	W.M.G
			Cpl Knust, Bdy L (since [illegible]) LCpl E Clark, B T (def sic) " [illegible] Chaloners 5 " J Upton 3 (non [illegible]) " J Green D 7 " F Seville C	
	19/5		During the time the Battalion [illegible] in Divisional [illegible] on a [illegible] was carried out. Considerable work on a [illegible] given by [illegible]	B/M.G
		5pm	The 7th Bn was relieved by the 2nd [illegible] Bn and on Sy [illegible] Brigade [illegible] dropped along the [illegible] from our [illegible] the Hindenburg was littered	

WAR DIARY
or
INTELLIGENCE SUMMARY

Army Form C. 2118

Place	Date	Hour	Summary of Events and Information	Remarks and references to Appendices
HAPLINCOURT	14/8	5 am	Bn marched to VILLERS-FAUCON (E 22 D) in support of the 2nd Canadian Division who were attacking.	M.N.R.
VILLERS-FAUCON	29/8	9 a.m.	K.S.O.B. Baker Hughes were notified of readiness. Bakers Coys B, C + D Companies moved to SAUBCOURT F.9.d.4.B. H.Q'rs moved into BROWN LINE at E.15.A. pushing	W.N.B
SAUBCOURT	29/8 30/8	pm	Digging and wiring of trenches E of EPIHY (F.1.A)	W.N.R.
SAUBCOURT	30/8	6 a.m.	Bn marched to bank E of EQUANCOURT and bivouacked at V.11.A.2.2 (Ref 57 c NE) 20 Fighting Strength Officers 22 N.C.O.s and Oskers 473	W.N.R.

M. Donoghue 2 Lnt
Comdg 16 Durham and Oskers

Army Form C. 2118

WAR DIARY
or
INTELLIGENCE SUMMARY
(Erase heading not required.)

Vol 5

5.W

2/6TH BN. THE SHERWOOD FORESTERS.

WAR DIARY

FOR

MONTH OF JUNE.

1917.

Army Form C. 2118.

WAR DIARY
or
INTELLIGENCE SUMMARY.
(Erase heading not required.)

Hour, Date, Place	Summary of Events and Information	Remarks and references to Appendices
EQUANCOURT 1-6-17	Fighting Strength Officers 20 Other Ranks 493	
Thurs	Battalion took over line from Q.12.a.5.5. to Q.11.d.5.5. (Ref 59°SE) from 12th Bn East Lancashire Regt. The 25th Lancashire Fus. were on the right and 1/7th Bn Lancs went through on the left. Battn Hd. established at Q.15.c.7.3. Whilst the Battalion was in the line the Germans twice shelled it and made nice 30 yards from its line. No Casualties were sustained owing to this.	W.R.B.
NETZ 5-6-17 when	The Battn went in support at METZ-EN-COUTURE (Q20.c) on being relieved by the 2/5th Bn Gloucester Regiment. Working parties were sent out every night to dig No 3 Communication Trench running from Q.1.c.5.6. to Q.1b.c.1.2.	W.R.B. W.R.B.

WAR DIARY
or
INTELLIGENCE SUMMARY.
(Erase heading not required.)

Army Form C. 2118.

Hour, Date, Place	Summary of Events and Information	Remarks and references to Appendices
METZ 11-6-17 5 pm	The Battalion marched to Camp at EQUANCOURT in Army reserve by the 2/5th South Staffordshire Regt.	1st N.B.
EQUANCOURT 17/6/17	From 11/6/17 until 21/6/17 the Brigade was in Divisional Reserve. Training was carried out in movements over ground to the new.	
17/6/17 9.30am	Draft of 35 Other Ranks joined the Battalion from the 2nd Battalion.	
17/6/17 6.30pm	Inspection of the Battalion by Major Gen L.J. Bowen C.B. (M.G.A) C.	1st N.B.
19/6/17 2.30pm	The Battalion Rain Meeting	
19/6/17	Brigade Sports	1st N.B.
20/6/17	Brigade Rifle Meeting	1st N.B.
21-6-17 7.30pm	The Battalion took over the front line from R7 A.5.2 to R7 A.4.6 from	1st N.B.

(73989) W4141—463. 400,000. 9/14. H.&J.,Ltd. Forms/C. 2118/10.

Army Form C. 2118.

WAR DIARY
or
INTELLIGENCE SUMMARY.
(Erase heading not required.)

Hour, Date, Place	Summary of Events and Information	Remarks and references to Appendices
BEAUCAMP 21.6.17	On 21/s Leicestershire Regt. The 1/4th Northampton 2/4th Infantry were on the Right and 1/4th Oxon and Bucks Infantry on the Left. Battn HQ was established at Q.18.b.9.8. During the time 2 prisoners were captured by the Rataluns. These belonged to the 3rd Bn. 31 or 2 Regt. Casualties. Lieut. L. Rigsby Killed in action 3. Other Ranks do 2/Lt. N. Minshu Wounded in action 9 Ranks do " Other Ranks 17 Other Ranks 455 Infantry Brigade HQ [signature]	

ORIGINAL

WAR DIARY

2/6TH BN. THE SHERWOOD FORESTERS.

JULY 1917.

Army Form C. 2118

WAR DIARY
or
INTELLIGENCE SUMMARY
(Erase heading not required.)

Instructions regarding War Diaries and Intelligence Summaries are contained in F.S. Regs., Part II. and the Staff Manual respectively. Title Pages will be prepared in manuscript.

Place	Date	Hour	Summary of Events and Information	Remarks and references to Appendices
July 1917 Q.4.18 & 5.8. Ref. 57c SE	1/7/17		Fighting Strength - Officers 17. O.R. 450.	AB
	2/7/17	2am	Batln relieved by 2/5 London Foresters northwards into Brigade Reserve on DESSART WOOD. Batln H.Q. established at W.1.a.2.8. (Ref. 57c S.E.)	AB
	2/7/17		The whole Bn engaged on Working Parties whilst in Brigade Reserve.	AB
DESSART WOOD	2/7/17 to 8/7/17	9am	Batln marched to O.35.d.7.7. Ref 57c S.W. on the relief of the Division by 58th Division. 2/6 th Bn. London Regt. relieved 2/6 Bn. Sherwood Foresters 57th Division withdrawn into Army Reserve and Passed from III Corps IV Army to IV Corps 3rd Army.	AB
O.35.d.7.7	10/7/17		Training of Division proceeded in accordance with S.S.152. Appendix XIII	AB
	19/7/17		Brigade Tactical Exercise. Trench to Trench Attack over old BRITISH and GERMAN Trenches E of SAILLY - SAILLISEL. U.8.d.	AB
	23/7/17	8am		
	24/7/17	9am	Divisional Tactical Scheme No.1. Trench to Trench Attack over old BRITISH and GERMAN Trenches between LE TRANSLOY and SAILLY - SAILLISEL. U.1.	AB
	31/7/17	8am	One Company Field Firing at LIGNY - THILLOY Range N.9.a.5.1 — N.15.a.5.2.	AB
	31/7/17		Fighting Strength - Officers 11. O.R. 480.	AB

July. 31st 1917.

[Signature] Lt. Colonel,
Commdg. 2/6th Bn. The Sherwood Foresters.

ORIGINAL

Vol 7

2nd/6th Bn. SHERWOOD FORESTERS.

WAR DIARY,

AUGUST – 1917.

7.W

Army Form C. 2118

WAR DIARY
or
INTELLIGENCE SUMMARY
(Erase heading not required.)

Instructions regarding War Diaries and Intelligence Summaries are contained in F. S. Regs., Part II. and the Staff Manual respectively. Title Pages will be prepared in manuscript.

Place	Date	Hour	Summary of Events and Information	Remarks and references to Appendices
LE MESNIL 0.35 Central 17 57c S.W.	1/8		Fighting Strength Officers 14 Other Ranks 480	W.V.R.
	2/8/17		The Battn was in Rest Camp at LE MESNIL during which time training was carried out. Musketry, Rifle meetings & Boxing Competitions	W.V.R.
	3/8/17		do	W.V.R.
	4/8/17		8 hour Field Firing at LIGNY TILLOY	W.V.R.
	7/8/17		do	
	9/8/17		do	
	11/8/17		Div Tactical exercise, March to trench attack at LE TRANSLOY	W.V.R.
	15/8/17		Battn. fell back on trenches at U.12.d.50,75. carried out on 1/8 to 4/8 bomb under Capt. J.B. Stone	W.V.R.

1875 Wt. W593/826 1,000,000 4/15 J.B.C. & A. A.D.S.S./Forms/C. 2118.

WAR DIARY
or
INTELLIGENCE SUMMARY
(Erase heading not required.)

Army Form C. 2118

Place	Date	Hour	Summary of Events and Information	Remarks and references to Appendices
LE MESNIL O 35 b and S.7 c.S.W.	18/5/17		Brigade Indoor Exercise. Sunnah to launch attack by night at SAILLY SAILLISEL.	10-V-E
	24	6am	Batta moved by Motor Buses to LE SARS and from there by march route to MARTINSART (NIOC 3.B.ALBERT sheet)	10-N-E
	31	6am	Batta marched to BEAUCOURT station + entrained for HAZEBROUCK and from there to L2 & S.S. sheet 27 and K18 locap Hua.	10-N-E
			Fighting Strength Officers 18 Other Ranks 816.	

H. Hoar
Lieut. Col.
Cdg. 2/6 L.B. Sherwood Foresters.

Army Form C. 2118.

ORIGINAL

WAR DIARY
or
INTELLIGENCE SUMMARY

2/6 Bn. SHERWOOD FORESTERS.

WAR DIARY

SEPTEMBER 1917.

WAR DIARY or INTELLIGENCE SUMMARY

Army Form C. 2118

Place	Date	Hour	Summary of Events and Information	Remarks and references to Appendices
N. OF WINNEZEELE J.2.b.8.8 (Sheet 27)	1.9.17 to 19.9.17		Fighting Strength :- Officers 18. O.R's. 816. Training in accordance with 5th Army letter S.G 840/7 dated 24.8.17.	
FORGE L.7.d.b.3 (Sheet 27)	20.9.17 to 23.9.17		Marched from J.2.b.88 to L.7.d.b.3, and arrived there at 12 noon. The Battn. was billeted, and coy training was carried out.	
VLAMERTINGHE H.11.a.8.3 (Sheet 28)	23.9.17 H.24.9.17 10.6 12 noon		Marched to H.11.b.8.3, and arrived in a temporary camp for the night. Practised attack which was carried out at 5.50 a.m. Sept 26th.	
		6 p.m.	Battn. marched to trenches. Fighting strength 21 Officers. 609 Other Ranks. All training declens of 5 Offs and 108 Other Ranks were left behind at H.Q. 2.nd Stores.	
		10.0 p.m.	Relieved 2/5th South Staffs in front line running from CRAVENSTAFEL ROAD (D.13.d.80.85) to DOWNING TRENCH (D.14.q.35.40)	

WAR DIARY
or
INTELLIGENCE SUMMARY
(Erase heading not required.)

Army Form C. 2118

Place	Date	Hour	Summary of Events and Information	Remarks and references to Appendices
	25/9/17	4 to 0.30pm	Artillery practised barrage for operations on the 26th. Rather fairly heavily shelled. 2 O.R's wounded. Gased working off positions.	AB
	26/9/17	5.50 am	After heavy artillery barrage Battn. left its position, with 1/4th S.F. on the left and the 1/5th Bttn. on the right. The objective which was from D.1 + 3 inclusive to GRAFENSTAFEL ROAD (exclusive) was reached about 7.30 a.m. A number of prisoners were taken.	AB
	27/9/17	8 p.m	The enemy shelled our positions during the day, shelled heavily during the day. Relieved by 2/5th Bn. S.F. in the front line, who had held the 2nd objective.	AB
	28/9/17 29/9/17	9am	Battn relieved by the 1/4 Lincs and took up position in the Gold Redoubt front line in the rear of WIELTJE. Total Casualties 11 Off's 220 O.R's.	AB

R. B. Rickman. Major.
Cdg 1/8th Bn. The Sherwood Foresters.

ORIGINAL

Vol 9

WAR DIARY.
2/6th Bn. The Sherwood Foresters.
October 1917.

G.W.

Army Form C. 2118.

WAR DIARY
or
INTELLIGENCE SUMMARY

(Erase heading not required.)

Place	Date	Hour	Summary of Events and Information	Remarks and references to Appendices
			Fighting Strength:- 8 Officers, 23 Officers, 139 Other Ranks	
WIELTJE	1.10.17	4 p.m.	Relieved in Old British Front line, WIELTJE and marched to Camp, VLAMERTINGHE. H.Q. & 4.5 (Sheet 28). In the Fifth Army (II Anzac Corps).	
VLAMERTINGHE	2.10.17	8.5 a.m.	Entrained VLAMERTINGHE Station. Proceeded by rail to THIENNES. Marched to BOESEGHEM, where the Battn. billeted. (Ref map. HAZEBROUCK 5A) In the First Army (XI Corps).	
BOESEGHEM	3.10.17	11.0 a.m.	Battn. inspected on parade by G.O.C. 59th Division.	
	4.10.17		Training carried out - close order drill. etc.	
	5.10.17	9.45 a.m.	Battn. proceeded by bus to S.E. of THEROUANNE - from this point proceeded by march route to COYECQUE. Battn. billeted. In First Army Special Reserve Area. Additional Specialists commenced training carried out. Specialist Training.	
COYECQUE	6.10.17 to 9.10.17			
	10.10.17	8.30 a.m.	Marched to FIEFS. Battn. billeted in CHATEAU.	
FIEFS	11.10.17	9.0 a.m.	Marched to TANGRY. Battn. H.Q.'s and 1 Company billeted in TANGRY - remaining 3 Coys. billeted in SAINES-LES-PERNES.	
TANGRY	12.10.17	9.0 a.m.	Marched to BARLIN. Battn. billeted.	
BARLIN	13.10.17	9.0 a.m.	Marched to GOUY SERVINS. Arrived 1.0 p.m. Battn. billeted in Chateau. Brigade in Divisional Reserve.	

Army Form C. 2118.

WAR DIARY
or
INTELLIGENCE SUMMARY
(Erase heading not required.)

Instructions regarding War Diaries and Intelligence Summaries are contained in F. S. Regs., Part II. and the Staff Manual respectively. Title Pages will be prepared in manuscript.

Place	Date	Hour	Summary of Events and Information	Remarks and references to Appendices
GOUY SERVINS	19.10.17		Training of Battn. carried out. Training of additional specialist resumed	
	20.10.17			
	21.10.17	5 p.m.	Battn. entrained on light Railway GOUY-SERVINS. Detrained at LA COULOTTE and relieved 2/4th Bn Lincolnshire Regt in front line.	
AVION	22.10.17		Occupied front line - N 25 b 5.2 to N 33 c 1.9 (sheet LENS CANAL - 3rd EDITION) Battn H.Q. at LA COULOTTE N 31 C 7 3.	
	25.10.17		Draft of 66 Other Ranks arrived from 12th Bn. Sherwood Foresters.	
	26.10.17		Enemy raid on advanced night post repulsed. 1 enemy killed and captured. Our casualties 3 slightly wounded.	
	29.10.17	9.0 p.m.	Battn relieved & moved to Support line. Battn H. Q. established at S.6. Central	
	31.10.17		Total casualties - 3 O.R's killed, 11 O.R's wounded. Fighting Strength:- Officers 31 Other Ranks 810	

Acland Major.
Lodgg 6th Bn. Sherwood Foresters.

ORIGINAL

WAR DIARY.

2/6th BN SHERWOOD FORESTERS.

NOVEMBER 1917

WAR DIARY or INTELLIGENCE SUMMARY.

Army Form C. 2118.

(Erase heading not required.)

Hour, Date, Place		Summary of Events and Information	Remarks and references to Appendices
1.11.17		Fighting Strength :- Officers 31 Other Ranks 810	AB
1.11.17 to 6.11.17	AVION	Battn. reoccupied British Support Line. Battn. H.Qrs. S.6. Central (LENS CANAL 3rd Edition).	AB
10 a.m. 7.11.17	CARENCY	Battn. moved from Support Line to ALBERTA CAMP. X.17.a.8.3. (Sheet 36 B)	AB
8.11.17 to 13.11.17	do.	Battn. on Working Parties.	AB AB
9.0 a.m. 14.11.17	DUISANS	Left CARENCY and marched to DUISANS. L.8.6. (Sheet 51c).	AB
15.11.17 to 18.11.17	do.	Battn. training carried out. Reserve Signallers, Lewis Gunners etc. under Specialists, training.	AB AB
5.0 p.m. 19.11.17	HENDECOURT	Left DUISANS for No. 3 Camp, HENDECOURT.	AB
Ref. Map. 57c			
9.0 p.m. 21.11.17	GOMIECOURT	Left HENDECOURT for GOMIECOURT. A.28.b.5.3. Arrived 12 M.N.	AB
1.0 p.m. 23.11.17 to 25.11.17	do.	Battn. marched to ACHIET-LE-GRAND (G.10.c.) Entrained for FINS, (W.12.C) and marched to EQUANCOURT. (W.10.d.1.7) where Battn. billeted.	AB
6.0 p.m. 25.11.17	QUEENS CROSS	Battn. marched from EQUANCOURT to QUEENS CROSS. Q.28.d.4.4. Attached to 6th Division.	AB
1.0 p.m. 26.11.17		Marched to Hindenburg Support Line. In trenches R.1.a.4.3. to R.1.c.8.4.	AB
27.11.17		Battn. on Working Parties.	AB

Army Form C. 2118.

WAR DIARY
or
INTELLIGENCE SUMMARY.
(Erase heading not required.)

Instructions regarding War Diaries and Intelligence Summaries are contained in F.S. Regs., Part II. and the Staff Manual respectively. Title pages will be prepared in manuscript.

Hour, Date, Place		Summary of Events and Information	Remarks and references to Appendices
10.0 p.m.	28.11.17. QUEEN'S CROSS	Marched to QUEEN'S CROSS, a.28.d.4.4.	AB—F AB—F
1.30 p.m.	29.11.17.	Battn. marched to Old British line R.7.d. Commenced to dig defensive line HIGHLAND RIDGE Pt. 4 Pt. Moved to dugouts 20th Division — HINDENBURG line A.16.6.	AB—F
	30.11.17.	Battalion in reserve. Fighting Strength. Officers. 32 Other Ranks 806.	AB—F

A C Clarke Lt. Col
Cdg. 1/6th Bn. The Seaforth Boaters

Operations of 2/6th. Sherwood Foresters.
30.11.17 to 3.12.17.

Map Ref. C.T.S.(214)
Nov. 1917.

On the evening of 30.11.17., the Battalion was ordered by 6th. Div. (to which it had been attached), to move to VILLERS PLOUICH for attachment to 20th. Division.

G.O.C. 59th. Brigade instructed us to proceed to HINDENBURG LINE in R.10.d. & R.16.b., to be in Reserve to 11th. Battn. K.R.R. The Battn. occupied the Line by 01.00 hrs. on 1.12.17, getting into touch with 12th. Div. on the right, & 11th. K.R.R. on the left. At daybreak on 1.12.17., a Bosch aeroplane came over our Lines & the enemy opened with Artillery fire on the whole Area, paying special attention to the sunken roads; the shelling was more or less continuous until about 15.00 hrs.

The 12th. Div., who were holding the front line on the right, were heavily attacked at this time; some of this garrison withdrew, & fell back to the sunken road at R.16.b.6.2, (our right flank). In order to deal with a possibilty of this flank being threatened, the right forward Company was ordered to moved half his men, to the sunken road at R.16.b.3.2., to face SOUTH, with instructions to form a defensive flank; this position was found to be untenable, owing to the heavy shell fire; the half company was therefore moved to occupy a trench at R.16.a.5.0.

The situation did not alter during the night except that 12th. Division in front line, was relieved by parts of 61st. Div.

When the right forward Company was ordered to form a defensive flank, one platoon of the Reserve Company was ordered to occupy a trench at R.10.c.7.5., which had a good field of fire, over the ground over which the enemy would have to advance.

~~Xxxxxxxxxx~~ O.C.11th. K.R.R. was informed of what had been done, & also of the situation on the right flank; he ordered the C.O. to report to G.O.C.59th. Bde., to explain what was happening & at the same time ask for instructions; this was done & the instructions received were, "the HINDENBURG LINE is to be held at all costs". The situation did not change during the night. Early on the morning of 2.12.17, the enemy again heavily

(1)

bombarded our positions, & this continued until the afternoon, when he again attacked in force from the SOUTH; this attack succeeded on the right as far as the front line was concerned, as it caused the front line to fall back to the sunken road at R.16.b.6.2. & the trench occupied by this Battn. at R.16.b.3.2. At this stage the enemy came into view of our Lewis Guns & Rifles; effective fire was brought to bear, & their advance was checked. This held up his attack, & the further withdrawal stopped.
The Lewis Guns were the cause of inflicting considerable loss on the enemy, as soon as he came into view.
By this time the two Companies on the threatened flank had suffered many casualties. They were greatly impeded in their operations by the troops, which had been driven in from the front line; these troops which numbered between 150 & 200 men remained in the trenches occupied by the two right Companies of this Battn., & Lieut. Sampson of this Battn., had the greatest difficulty in getting them to re-organise. They were however eventually got together & sent back to try & regain a portion of the lost ground.
It was entirely owing to the gallant conduct of Lt. Sampson & commanding "C" Company, & 2/ Lt. Archer, commanding "B" Company that the HINDENBURG LINE was not lost at this point.
At dusk the enemy worked down the evacuated trenches to the sunken road at R.16.b.3.2. & established a Bombing post there.
He placed a Machine Gun at R.16.b.7.4.
This was the situation when the Battn. was relieved by 2/6th. Warwicks on the night of 2/3rd. Dec.

Meanwhile on the Left front on I.12.17, the enemy were making bombing attacks up the C.T's.; they succeeded in driving a portion of the garrison back. In response to a request from a Company Commander of another Battn., one platoon was sent forward to re-inforce. Owing to complete absence of bombs, it was not possible to drive the enemy back the way he had come; all bombs, both our own & also salvaged German bombs had been collected & used long before. One platoon from the Left Company was ordered to move forward to assist in checking the enemy advance, & another platoon was ordered from the Reserve Company, to re-place them in the HINDENBURG Line.

On Dec. 2nd., the enemy made further attempts to advance along the C.T's, & was successful. Absence of bombs again made it impossible to deal with the situation in a satisfactory manner. The remaining Platoon of the Reserve Company was sent forward on the left, as the Company Commander in the forward position, was of the opinion that the enemy could not be held up.

This platoon took up a position in the sunken road at R.10.d.3.8. & R.10.d.3.6., thus covering any attempt of the enemy to gain possession of the sunken road at R.10.d.1.8.

This was the situation when the Battn. was relieved at 04.25 HRS. on 3.12.17.

During these three days, our rations & mail arrived just as usual; the Transport Lines were back at Equancourt, & the nightly journey to the Dump was full of thrills, owing to the route that was followed, being through Gouzecourt, which was at the time very close to the Bosch Lines.

The casualties suffered by the Battn. during the three days were:-

   Officers .... 3.
   Other Ranks 122

The G.O.C. 20th. Div. very kindly thanked the Battn. for their services, & their help whilst they were attached.

(3)

The HINDENBURG LINE in which we found ourselves, faced North East, & was as elsewhere enormously wide, & of course faced the "wrong way"; further the slope of the ground was towards the enemy, & this made the position an easy target for his guns.

The deep dug-outs, of which there were several, also faced the wrong way; one of them was used as the R.A.P. & it added to the difficulties of the M.O. & his S.Bs. to have the entrance continually pounded by shells.

There had been a good deal of rain, & the state of the trenches in many places, particularly the C.Ts., was such that it was almost impossible to move about.

There was a complete lack of Artillery support on this portion of the Line, & owing to there being no organised communications, except by runner, we could not get into touch.

On being relieved the Battn. moved back to Beauchamp Ridge, & during the next day or so rejoined its own Brigade, in the neighbourhood of RIBECOURT.

Had the Bosch continued the attack & made a really determined effort on Dec. 1st. & 2nd. it is difficult to see how he could have failed to cut off the Salient we held round about Flesquiers, as there were few troops close at hand to oppose him.

OPERATIONS of 2/6th Sherwood Foresters.
30.11.17 to 3.12.17.
Supplied by Lt.-Colonel A.C.Clarke. T.D.

Map Ref. C.T.S. (214)

November 1917.   On the evening of 30.11.17 the battalion was ordered by 6th Division (to which it had been attached), to move to Villers Plouich for attachment to 20th Division.

G.O.C. 59th Brigade instructed us to proceed to Hindenburg Line in R.10.d and R.16.b., to be in reserve to 11th Battalion K.R.R.C. The battalion occupied the line by 01.00 hrs. on 1.12.17, getting into touch with 12th Division on the right, and 11/K.R.R.C. on the left. At daybreak on 1.12.17, a Boche aeroplane came over our lines and the enemy opened with artillery fire on the whole area, paying special attention to the sunken roads; the shelling was more or less continuous until about 15.00 hrs.

The 12th Division, who were holding the front line on the right, were heavily attacked at this time; some of this garrison withdrew, and fell back to the sunken road at R.16.b.6.2 (our right flank). In order to deal with a possibility of this flank being threatened, the right forward company was ordered to move half his men, to the sunken road at R.16.b.3.2. to face south, with instructions to form a defensive flank; this position was found to be untenable owing to the heavy shell fire; the half company was therefore moved to occupy a trench at R.16.a.5.0.

The situation did not alter during the night, except that 12th Division in frontline was relieved by parts of 61st Division. When the right forward company was ordered to form a defensive flank, one platoon of the reserve company was ordered to occupy a trench at

R.10.c.7.5., which had a good field of fire over the ground over which the enemy would have to advance.

O.C. 11/K.R.R.C. was informed of what had been done, and also of the situation on the right flank; he ordered the C.O. to report to G.O.C. 59th Bde., to explain what was happening and at the same time ask for instructions; this was done and the instructions received were, "the Hindenburg Line is to be "held at all costs." The situation did not change during the night.

Early on the morning of 2.12.17 the enemy again heavily bombarded our positions, and this continued until the afternoon, when he again attacked in force from the south; this attack succeeded on the right as far as the front line was concerned, as it caused the front line to fall back to the sunken road at R.16.b.6.2. and the trench occupied by this battalion at R.16.b.3.2. At this stage the enemy came into view of our Lewis guns and rifles; effective fire was brought to bear and their advance was checked. This held up his attack and the further withdrawal stopped. The Lewis guns were the cause of inflicting considerable loss on the enemy, as soon as he came into view.

By this time the two companies on the threatened flank had suffered many casualties. They were greatly impeded in their operations by the troops, which had been driven in from the front line; these troops which numbered between 150 and 200 men remained in the trenches occupied by the two right companies of this battalion, and Lieut. Sampson of this battn. had the greatest difficulty in getting them to reorganise. They were however eventually got together and sent back to try and regain a portion of the lost ground.

It was entirely owing to the gallant conduct of Lieut. Sampson and commanding "C" Coy., and 2/Lieut. Archer, commanding "B" Coy. that the Hindenburg Line was not lost at this point.

At dusk the enemy worked down the evacuated trenches to the sunken road at R.16.b.3.2. and established a bombing post there. He placed a machine gun at R.16.b.7.4.

This was the situation when the battalion was relieved by 2/6th Warwicks on the night of 2/3rd Dec.

Meanwhile on the left front on 1.12.17 the enemy were making bombing attacks up the C.T's; they succeeded in driving a portion of the garrison back. In response to a request from a company commander of another battalion, one platoon was sent forward to reinforce. Owing to complete absence of bombs it was not possible to drive the enemy back the way he had come; all bombs, both our own and also salvaged German bombs had been collected and used along before. One platoon from the left company was ordered to move forward to assist in checking the enemy advance, and another platoon was ordered from the reserve company to replace them in the Hindenburg Line.

On 2nd December the enemy made further attempts to advance along the C.T's and was successful. Absence of bombs again made it impossible to deal with the situation in a satisfactory manner. The remaining platoon of the reserve company was sent forward on the left, as the company commander in the forward position was of the opinion that the enemy could not be held up. This platoon took up a position in the sunken road at R.10.d.3.8. and R.10.d.3.6., thus covering any attempt of the enemy to gain possession of the sunken road at R.10.d.1.8.

This was the situation when the battalion was relieved at 04.25 hrs. on 3.12.17.

During these three days, our rations and mail arrived just as usual, the transport lines were back at Equancourt, and the nightly journey to the dump was full of thrills, owing to the route that was followed, being through Gouzecourt, which was at the time very close to the Boche lines.

The casualties suffered by the battalion during the three days were:-

        Officers...........3
        Other Ranks......122.

The G.O.C. 20th Division very kindly thanked the battalion for their services, and their help whilst they were attacked.

The Hindenburg Line in which we found ourselves, faced north-east, and was as elsewhere enormously wide, and of course faced the "wrong way"; further the slope of the ground was towards the enemy, and this made the position an easy target for his guns.

The deep dug-outs, of which there were several, also faced the wrong way; one of them was used as the R.A.P, and it added to the difficulties of the M.O. and his S.B's to have the entrance continually pounded by shells.

There had been a good deal of rain, and the état of the trenches in many places, particularly the C.T's, was such that it was almost impossible to move about.

There was a complete lack of artillery support on this portion of the line, and owing to there being no organised communications, except by runner, we could not get into touch.

On being relieved the battalion moved back to Beauchamp Ridge, and during the next day or so rejoined its own brigade in the neighbourhood of Ribecourt.

Had the Boche continued the attack and made a really determined effort on December 1st and 2nd, it is difficult to see how he could have failed to cut off the salient we held round about Flesquiers, as there were few troops close at hand to oppose him.

- - - - - - - - -

WAR DIARY.
FOR
DEC, 1917.
2/6TH. BN. SHERWOOD FORESTERS.

178/59

ORIGINAL

WAR DIARY or INTELLIGENCE SUMMARY

Army Form C. 2118.

Place	Date	Hour	Summary of Events and Information	Remarks and references to Appendices
LA VACQUERIE R.16. (Special Sheet 57°N.E.S.E. and 57°N.W.S.W.)	1.12.17	1 am	Fighting strength — Officers — 32 Other Ranks — 806 Attacked 20th Division in Hindenburg Line R.10.d and R.16.b.t (Ref. Special Sheet 57°N.E.S.E. and 57°N.W.S.W.) Battalion in Reserve to 11th & 13th K.R.R. The 12th Division who were holding front line on our right were heavily attacked about 3 p.m. Some of this Division fell back to Sunken Road R.16.b.62 (our right flank). Half of our right flank company moved to Sunken Road R.16.b.32, facing North to form defensive flank. This position was untenable and the half company were moved to trench at R.16.a.5.0. One platoon of our Reserve Company moved to trench at R.10.c.4.5. On our left front enemy made bombing attacks up O.T's and succeeded in driving back a portion of the front line. We sent up 1 Platoon to reinforce, but owing to absence of bombs it was unable to drive enemy back. One platoon of left company moved forward to assist in checking enemy advance. One platoon from Reserve Company replaced the platoon heavily bombarded in early morning. Enemy attacked in the afternoon on our right flank and caused front line to fall back to Sunken Road at R.16.b.6.2. and trench occupied by our Battalion at R.16.b.3.2. Our Lewis guns and rifle fire held up his attack at this point. On our left front the enemy made attempts to bomb up O.T's and succeeded in getting into the trench. Remaining Platoon of Reserve Company was sent forward and held up a position in Sunken Road at R.10.d.3.6, and R.10.d.3 & 8 covering any attempt of the enemy to gain possession of Sunken Road at R.10.d.1.8.	 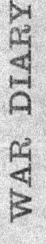
	2.12.17			

Army Form C. 2118.

WAR DIARY
or
INTELLIGENCE SUMMARY.
(Erase heading not required.)

Instructions regarding War Diaries and Intelligence Summaries are contained in F. S. Regs., Part II. and the Staff Manual respectively. Title pages will be prepared in manuscript.

Place	Date	Hour	Summary of Events and Information	Remarks and references to Appendices
LA VACQUERIE	3.12.17	4.25 a.m.	Battalion relieved by 2/6th Warwicks. Moved to VILLERS PLUICH.	A/B
		10.0 a.m	Moved to MOLE TRENCH in L.31.a.10.3 near RIBECOURT.	A/B
		10.30 p.m.	Moved to trenches in Q.4 at TRESCAULT.	A/B
TRESCAULT	5.12.17 to 8.12.17		Battalion in reserve at Q.4.	A/B
FLESQUIRES	9.12.17	6.0 p.m	Battalion moved up to FLESQUIRES.	A/B
	10.12.17	1.30 a.m	Relieved 2/5 Lincolns in front line K18.a.t. (MOEUVRES- Special Sheet)	A/B
	11.12.17 to 13.12.17		Battalion occupied front line in K18.a.t. (MOEUVRES- Special Sheet).	A/B
	14.12.17	2 a.m.	Relieved by 2/5 South Staffs.	A/B
FLESQUIRES	14.12.17 to 16.12.17		Battalion occupied Reserve line in K27.a. (MOEUVRES- Special Sheet)	A/B
	17.12.17	8 p.m.	Battalion relieved by 2/5th Lincolns. Marched to BERTINCOURT. Battalion billeted.	A/B
BERTINCOURT	18.12.17 to 20.12.17		Company Training	A/B
ROCQUIGNY	21.12.17		Battalion marched to ROCQUIGNY. Billeted in huts for the night.	A/B
BEAULENCOURT	22.12.17 to 25.12.17		Battalion marched to BEAULENCOURT. Billeted in huts. Battalion Training	A/B
			Battalion marched to BAPAUME. Entrained at BAPAUME, detrained at HOUVIN.	A/B
MAGNICOURT	26.12.17 to 31.12.17		Battalion marched to MAGNICOURT. Battalion and Company Training.	A/B

Army Form C. 2118.

WAR DIARY
or
INTELLIGENCE SUMMARY.
(Erase heading not required.)

Instructions regarding War Diaries and Intelligence Summaries are contained in F.S. Regs., Part II. and the Staff Manual respectively. Title pages will be prepared in manuscript.

Place	Date	Hour	Summary of Events and Information	Remarks and references to Appendices
	31.12.17		Fighting Strength - Officers - 27. Other Ranks - 729.	AB I

AB Captain
for Lieut. Col.,
Comg. 2/6th Bn. the Sherwood Foresters.

ORIGINAL.

Vol 12

2/6th. Battalion Sherwood Foresters.

WAR DIARY.
JANUARY - 1918.

12.W.

Army Form C. 2118.

WAR DIARY
or
INTELLIGENCE SUMMARY.
(Erase heading not required.)

Instructions regarding War Diaries and Intelligence Summaries are contained in F. S. Regs., Part II. and the Staff Manual respectively. Title pages will be prepared in manuscript.

Place	Date	Hour	Summary of Events and Information	Remarks and references to Appendices
MAGNICOURT-SOUS-CANCH. H.10.d (Sh.51c)	1/1/18 to 3/1/18		Fighting Strength :- 27 Officers. 729 O.Rs. Battalion without Brigade. Battalion & Company training carried out, also Training of Additional Specialists.	
	12/1/18		Inspection by G.O.C. 59th Division, as follows :-	
		9.30am	"A" Company	
		10.20 am	"B" Company	
		11.10 am	"C" Company	
		12.0 Noon	"D" Company	
		12.50pm	Transport	
	20/1/18	11.0 am	Presentation of Military Medal Ribbons by G.O.C. 59th Division to the following :- 201,612 Pte. Felce W.L.B. 241,765 L/Sgt. Palmer A.	
	22/1/18	10.0 am	Battalion Tactical Exercise.	
	29/1/18	9 am	Letter "A" Company moved into billets at MONTS-EN-TERNOIS, B.26.c. (S'1c) Draft of 5 Officers & 143 O.Rs. arrived from 2/8 & 2/5 Bn Sherwood Foresters.	
	30/1/18		Fighting Strength. 32 Offrs. 936 O.Rs.	

A.K. Hodgkin Lieut.Col.
Comdg. 2/6 Bn. Sherwood Foresters,

ORIGINAL

WO/13

2/6 Bn. THE SHERWOOD FORESTERS.

WAR DIARY

FEBRUARY – 1918

13.W.

Army Form C. 2118.

WAR DIARY
or
INTELLIGENCE SUMMARY.
(Erase heading not required.)

Place	Date	Hour	Summary of Events and Information	Remarks and references to Appendices
MAGNICOURT-SUR-CANCHE H.10.d. (Sheet 51c)	1/2/18 to 4/2/18		Fighting Strength. 52 Offrs. 936 ORs. Battalion in 46th Brigade. Battalion & Company training carried out, also training of Battalion Specialists.	
H.H.d.	5/2/18	11.20 a.m.	Brigade inspected by G.O.C. VI h Corps.	
	5/2/18 to 7/2/18		Battalion & Company training carried out.	
GOUY-en-ARTOIS B.13.c. (51c)	8/2/18	10.15 a.m.	Battalion proceeded by March Route to GOUY-en-ARTOIS, B.13.c. (Sheet 51c).	
DURHAM CAMP S.11.a. (51c)	9/2/18	10.10 a.m.	Battalion proceeded by March Route to DURHAM CAMP, S.11.a. (Sheet 51c).	
MORY L'ABBAYE B.22.a. (57c)	10/2/18	10.0	Battalion proceeded by March Route to MORY L'ABBAYE, B.22.a. (Sheet 57c).	
	11/2/18		Battalion relieved 21st Middlesex Regiment in front line running from U.14.a.75.10. to U.20.b.40.80. Sheet 51B S.W.	
B.21.d. (Sheet 57c N.W.)	23/2/18	7 p.m.	Battalion relieved by 2/5th Sherwood Foresters, proceeded by March Route to NORTH CAMP, MORY, B.21.d.	
	24/2/18 to 25/2/18		Battalion on Working Parties.	
Sheet 51 B.S.W.	26.2.18	5.45 p.m.	Letter A.T.C. Companies proceeded to RAILWAY RESERVE (T.24.d.7.5.) to construct accommodation for Reserve Battalion in Brigade later.	
Sheet 51 C S.W.	28/2/18	6.0 p.m.	Battalion Headquarters letters B & D Companies proceeded to 25.6.3.4. Fighting Strength. 53 Offrs. 883 ORs.	

N.G. Horsburgh
Lieut. Col.,
Comg. 2/6 L.Bn. The Sherwood Foresters.

59th Division.
178th Infantry Brigade.

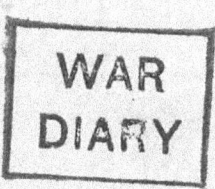

2/6th BATTALION

SHERWOOD FORESTERS.

MARCH 1 9 1 8

Narrative of Operations attached.

HQrs.
59th Division

Herewith War Diary for
month ending March 1918.
please.

K.B.———— Capt + adjt
for Lt. Col.
26.4.18.   Cdg 2/6th Bn. Sherwood Foresters.

ORIGINAL 128/9

2/7TH BN
2/6 — BN THE SHERWOOD FORESTERS.

WAR DIARY.

MARCH 1918.

Army Form C. 2118.

WAR DIARY
or
INTELLIGENCE SUMMARY.
(Erase heading not required.)

Instructions regarding War Diaries and Intelligence Summaries are contained in F. S. Regs., Part II. and the Staff Manual respectively. Title pages will be prepared in manuscript.

Place	Date	Hour	Summary of Events and Information	Remarks and references to Appendices
Sheet 57B. U.25.b.3.4.	1.3.18.		Battn contructing Reserve accommodation at U.25.b.3.4. Fighting Strength 53 Offs. 883 O.Rs	
"	2.3.18		Battn relieved by 23rd Bn. Northumberland Fusiliers, and marched to NORTH CAMP, MORY B.21.b.8.7 (Sheet 57c)	
NORTH CAMP MORY B.21.b.8.7	2.3.18 to 10.3.18		Battn on Working Parties on Reserve Line NOREUIL 6.9.b. (Sheet 57c).	
U.14.	11.3.18 to 20.3.18		Battn occupied front line in U.14 (Sheet 57C).	
U.14	21.3.18.		Very heavy enemy barrage on front line from 5.0 a.m. to 9.30 a.m. Enemy attacked at 9.30 a.m. Battn suffered very heavy casualties. Remainder of Battn. withdrawn to AYETTE F.6.C.3.3. (Sheet 57D)	
AYETTE	22.3.18 23.3.18		Battn. proceeded by March route to SENLIS V.10.d.8.4 (Sheet 57D)	
SENLIS.	24.3.18		Battn. proceeded by March route to ESBLER, NR BEAUCOURT.	
ESBLER	25.3.18		Battn. proceeded by March route to FIEFFES, NR CANDAS.	
FIEFFES	26.3.18		Battn. entrained at CANDAS, and detrained at LAPUGNOY. D.21.a.9.9 (Sheet 36 B) from this point proceeded by Bus to CAMBLIGNEUL W.14.d.2.4 (Sheet 36B).	
CAMBLIGNEUL	28.3.18		N.W. The King visited CAMBLIGNEUL	
"	30.3.18	2.0pm	Inspection of Battn by G.O.C. 59th Division. Fighting Strength 30 Offs. 627 O.Rs.	

ABrentney Capt Rach
for Lt. Col
Cdg 2/6th Bn. Sherwood Foresters.

Narrative of the German attack against the 2/6th
Battalion, Sherwood Foresters, on 21st
March, 1918.

The battalion went into the Line on the 9th March. From the first all ranks were acquainted with the fact that the Germans contemplated an offensive and that the battalion front was certain to be attacked if they carried it out, consequently everything possible was done to make the sector strong in defence ... I state this to show that there was no question of surprise.

The 7th Battalion Sherwood Foresters, the right battalion of the Division, linked up with the left battalion of the 6th Division, and the 2/6th Sherwood Foresters continued the line northwards, joining the right battalion of the 176th Brigade just south of BULLECOURT village.

The battalion was organised in depth: two companies in front of the RAILWAY RESERVE - holding advanced posts and the support line: two companies and battalion headquarters in RAILWAY RESERVE.

During the night 20/21st March my patrols were very vigilant, but they failed to notice anything unusual in No Man's Land. (After my capture, a German told me that the attacking troops were lying out in front of the trenches, having taken up their positions earlier in the night.

At 5 a.m. the enemy opened a terrific bombardment with guns of all calibres on to RAILWAY RESERVE, and the same time commenced shelling the posts in front of that line with trench mortars. The bombardment was continuous until 9 a.m. - except for a slight lull at 7 a.m. During the lull I was able to get touch with my posts. I found that the battalion had had few casualties and the situation was well in hand. I informed the brigade of the state of affairs. The bombardment commenced more intensely than ever and continued until 9 a.m. Simultaneously with the artillery lifting, the enemy infantry came forward. This attack was easily stopped, and the enemy was driven back to his own trenches.

For some time things were very quiet and I was able to make reconnaissance, and I found the situation at 9.45 a.m. as follows ... Three of my front posts were holding out; the supports on the left formed a protective flank from TANK AVENUE, but the supporting posts in the rear of the right company had apparently been knocked out by trench mortars fired from the apex. A considerable force of infantry was advancing in that direction and they appeared to have taken all the posts of the battalion on my right. About this time a number of stragglers from the 7th battalion came to my headquarters; these I collected and placed in my trenches. They informed me that the Germans had already taken their own battalion headquarters, and that their battalion was "done in" I was then isolated from the rear, and the enemy was working round my right. I reinforced my right, and as the men went along I explained the situation and told them to do their duty and hold on to the RAILWAY RESERVE at all costs as we were certain to be relieved when our counter-attack was made itself felt. At 10 a.m. my left company in RAILWAY RESERVE reported that the enemy was attacking in strong force from the direction of TANK AVENUE. I was able to reinforce this part of the line, where some extremely bitter fighting took place at close quarters. I was not able to communicate with this company after this, but we could see them holding on and fighting with bombs for some time. At 10.30 a.m. a force of the enemy moved round my flank and occupied SIDNEY AVENUE ... the whole of the RAILWAY EMBANKMENT was at this time enfiladed from the south by trench mortars and machine guns .. I was suffering very heavy losses and it was not possible to collect men to make a bayonet charge which I had ordered to be made.

The enemy after this bombing, eventually captured the trenches on the embankment up to the Regimental Aid Posts. He had also penetrated on my left. After collecting signallers, runners and servants, battalion headquarters fought (with practically no cover from the rear) until the ammunition was spent, and most of the officers and men were casualties. It was not until we were entirely surrounded that that part of the RAILWAY EMBANKMENT near Battalion Headquarters was taken by the enemy.

I am proud to state that all ranks fought splendidly, and it is difficult, where all did so well, to single out any individuals for special praise, but I should like to bring to your notice the names of the following officers and N.C.Os-

Captain S.A.Rogers, who commanded the left company in RAILWAY RESERVE, was killed after refusing to surrender. He led his company with great ability, and his personal example was magnificent.

Major A.C.Clarke, although wounded, worked a Lewis gun with much effect and on one occasion used it against a party of enemy who were forming up for attack and inflicted many casualties upon them. He did splendidly all through.

Sec.Lieut. D.St.Leger (R.F.A.) died of wounds the following day. This officer, after the lines of his battery had gone, used a rifle until he was so badly wounded that he was unable to stand. St.Leger was several times wounded, and even when his jaw had been shattered, remained cheerful. He was a real hero.

Sec.Lieut. H.Hickman, A/Adjutant, did well throughout the action and his work collecting stragglers was of great value. He personally destroyed all the correspondence and telephone-apparatus, so that nothing of importance fell into the hands of the enemy.

Sergt.Major - Holroyd set a fine example to us all. He voluntarily took up the task of organising ammunition for the last stand, and regardless of personal danger kept up a supply of bandoliers. This N.C.O's duty devotion to duty was magnificent.

Sergts.Parson and Mitchell were both killed in the discharge of duties for which they had specially volunteered.

Sec.Lieut.S.M.Johnson (being badly wounded), collected reports throughout the action, and his utter disregard of danger kept up the moral of the men. His work was of great importance and he kept going until he became unconscious.

                                      (Sd) H.S.Hodgkin, Lt.Col.
                                        (4th Dragoon Guards)
                                  Commanding 2/6th Sherwood Fors.

Copy of letter from Major A.C.Clarke. (2nd-in-Command, 2/6th Sherwood Foresters) to Br.-General T.W.Stansfield.)

January 14/19.

March 21st, 1918.

During the night 20/21st March, our artillery did a great deal of firing, but after 2 a.m. on 21st very few shells came over. Weather fine but misty.

5 a.m. Enemy bombardment opened - guns of all calibres being used against our Reserve trenches - Trench Mortars were chiefly used against our front and support lines. A large quantity of gas shells were used. All communications were destroyed as soon as the bombardment began. The shelling continued with great intensity until 9 a.m. From 7.15 to 9 a.m. hurricane bombardment. The front line was completely obliterated and considerable damage was done to the Reserve Line. "Battle positions" were manned soon after 5 a.m. As soon as it was light enough to see I went up to Post No.18 to find out what the situation was.

9 a.m. Enemy reported to be advancing. I at once went up to Post No.18 and saw the Bosche moving forward from his support line in 3 waves - 50 yards between each - a line of mopper's up followed the first wave. I then ran down to B.H.Q. dug-out to inform the C.O., and

9.20 a.m. on my way back to Post No.18, put up 2 S.O.S. rockets, one having been previously put up. The enemy on our immediate front moved slowly forward to the dead ground East of our front line - meanwhile I noticed large numbers of Bosche moving West, on the high ground - the spurs running East of Ecouste & Noreuil, north and south of us respectively. I at once ordered fire to be opened on them, they being some 800 - 1,000 yards away. There was no reply to our S.O.S. except a few heavies. Enemy barrage on Rly. Reserve still continued and men were continually hit. Owing to the formation of the two spurs mentioned, the enemy disappeared from view soon after fire was opened. I next saw the enemy moving forward from the dead ground in front of us and at once went down to inform the C.O., and returned (to) Post No.18 almost at the same time. Crowds of Bosche appeared on the high ground S. of us - 400 yards away, and these began to enfilade us with M.G's and rifle fire. We were also being enfiladed from the high ground North of us. I immediately ordered all available men to fire on the enemy South of us, as they were densely packed in large numbers (some 200 of them) at the same time I ordered a corporal to make his way back to Bde. H.Q. to inform them of the serious, not to say desperate, position we were in. I myself picked up a Lewis gun and got off 3 magazines at 400 yards - the gun then jammed. As soon as the high ground North & South of us had been secured, the Bosche in front of us advanced up to the Railway Embankment and lobbed bombs over. Heavy casualties had by this time been sustained from M.G's, Rifles and Bombs. When the L.G. jammed I picked up a rifle and continued to use this till I felt a tap on the shoulder and on looking up, saw a Bosche with rifle and bayonet standing over me.

(sgd) A.C.Clarke
Major.

Narrative of the German attack against the 2/6th
Battalion Sherwood Foresters on 21st.
March, 1918.

The Battalion went into the Line on the 9th. March. From the first all ranks were acquainted with the fact that the Germans contemplated an offensive and that the Battalion front was certain to be attacked if they carried it out, consequently everything possible was done to make the sector strong in defense ... I state this to show that there was no question of surprise.

The 7th. Battalion Sherwood Foresters, the right Battalion of the Division, linked up with the left Battalion of the 6th. Division, and the 2/6th Sherwood Foresters continued the Line northwards, joining the right Battalion of the 176th Brigade just south of BULLECOURT Village.

The Battalion was organized in depth: two Companies in front of the RAILWAY RESERVE - holding advanced posts and the support line: two companies and Battalion Headquarters in RAILWAY RESERVE.

During the night 20/21st. March my patrols were very vigilant, but they failed to notice anything unusual in No Man's Land. (After my capture, a German told me that the attacking troops were lying out in front of the trenches, having taken up their positions earlier in the night.

At 5 a.m. the enemy opened a terrific bombardment with guns of all calibres on to RAILWAY RESERVE, and the same time commenced shelling the posts in front of that line with trench mortars. The bombardment was continuous until 9 a.m. - except for a slight lull at 7 a.m. During the lull I was able to get touch with my posts. I found that the Battalion had had few casualties and the situation was well in hand. I informed the Brigade of the state of affairs. The bombardment commenced more intensely than ever and continued until 9 a.m. Simultaneously with the artillery lifting, the enemy infantry came forward. This attack was easily stopped, and the enemy was driven back to his own trenches.

For some time things were very quiet and I was able to make reconnaisance, and I found the situation at 9-45 a.m. as follows: .. three of my front posts were holding out; the supports on the left formed a protective flank from TANK AVENUE, but the supporting posts in the rear of the right company had aparently been knocked out by trench mortars fired from the apex. A considerable force of infantry was advancing in that direction and they appeared to have taken all the posts of the Battalion on my right. About this time a number of stragglers from the 7th. Battalion came to my Headquarters; these I collected and placed in my trenches. They informed that the Germans had already taken their own Battalion Headquarters, and that their Battalion was "done in". I was then isolated from the rear, and the enemy was working round my right. I reinforced my right, and as the men went along I explained the situation and told them to do their duty and hold on to the RAILWAY RESERVE at all costs as we were certain to be relieved when our counter-attack made itself felt. At 10 a.m. my left company in Railway RESERVE reported that the enemy was attacking in strong force from the direction of TANK AVENUE. I was able to reinforce this part of the line, where some extremely bitter fighting took place at close quarters. I was not able to communicate with this company after this, but we could see them holding on and fighting with bombs for some time. At 10-30 a.m. a force of the enemy moved round my flank and occupied SIDNEY AVENUE .. the whole of the RAILWAY EMBANKMENT was at this time enfiladed from the south by trench mortars and machine guns .. I was suffering very heavy losses and it was not possible to collect men to make a bayonet charge which I had ordered to be made.

H.S. Hodgkin L/Col
Comndg 2/6 Sherwood Foresters

Narrative of the German attack against the
2/6th Battalion Sherwood Foresters on 21st.
March 1918.

The enemy after this by bombing, eventually captured the trenches on the embankment up to the Regimental Aid posts. He had also penetrated on my left. After collecting signallers, runners and servants, Battalion Headquarters fought (with practically no cover from the rear) until the ammunition was spent, and most of the officers and men were casualties. It was not until we were entirely surrounded that that part of the RAILWAY EMBANKMENT near Battalion Headquarters was taken by the enemy.

I am proud to state that all ranks fought splendidly, and it is difficult, where all did so well, to single out any individuals for special praise, but I should like to bring to your notice the names of the following officers and N.C.Os:

Captain S.A.Rogers, who commanded the left company in Railway Reserve, was killed after refusing to surrender. He led his Company with great ability, and his personal example was magnificent.

Major A.C.Clarke, although wounded, worked a Lewis gun with much effect and on one occasion used it against a party of enemy who were forming up for attack and inflicted many casualties upon them. He did splendidly all through.

Sec.-Lieut. S.M.Johnson, (being badly wounded), collected reports throughout the action, and his utter disregard of danger kept up the moral of the men. His work was of great importance and he kept going until he became unconscious.

Sec.-Lieut. D. St.Leger (R.F.A.) died of wounds the following day. This officer, after the lines of his battery had gone, used a rifle until he was so badly wounded that he was unable to stand. St.Leger was several times wounded, and even when his jaw had been shattered, remained cheerful. He was a real hero.

Sec.-Lieut. H.Hickman, A/Adjutant, did well throughout the action and his work collecting stragglers was of great value. He personally destroyed all the correspondence and telephone-apparatus, so that nothing of importance fell into the hands of the enemy.

Sergt-Major - Holroyd set a fine example to us all. He voluntarily took up the task of organizing ammunition for the last stand, and regardless of personal danger kept up a supply of bandoliers. This N.C.O's devotion to duty was magnificent.

Sergts. Parson and Mitchell, were both killed in the discharge of duties for which they had specially volunteered.

H.S. Hodgkin Lt. Col.
(4th Dragoon Guards)
Commdg. 2/6th Sherwood Foresters

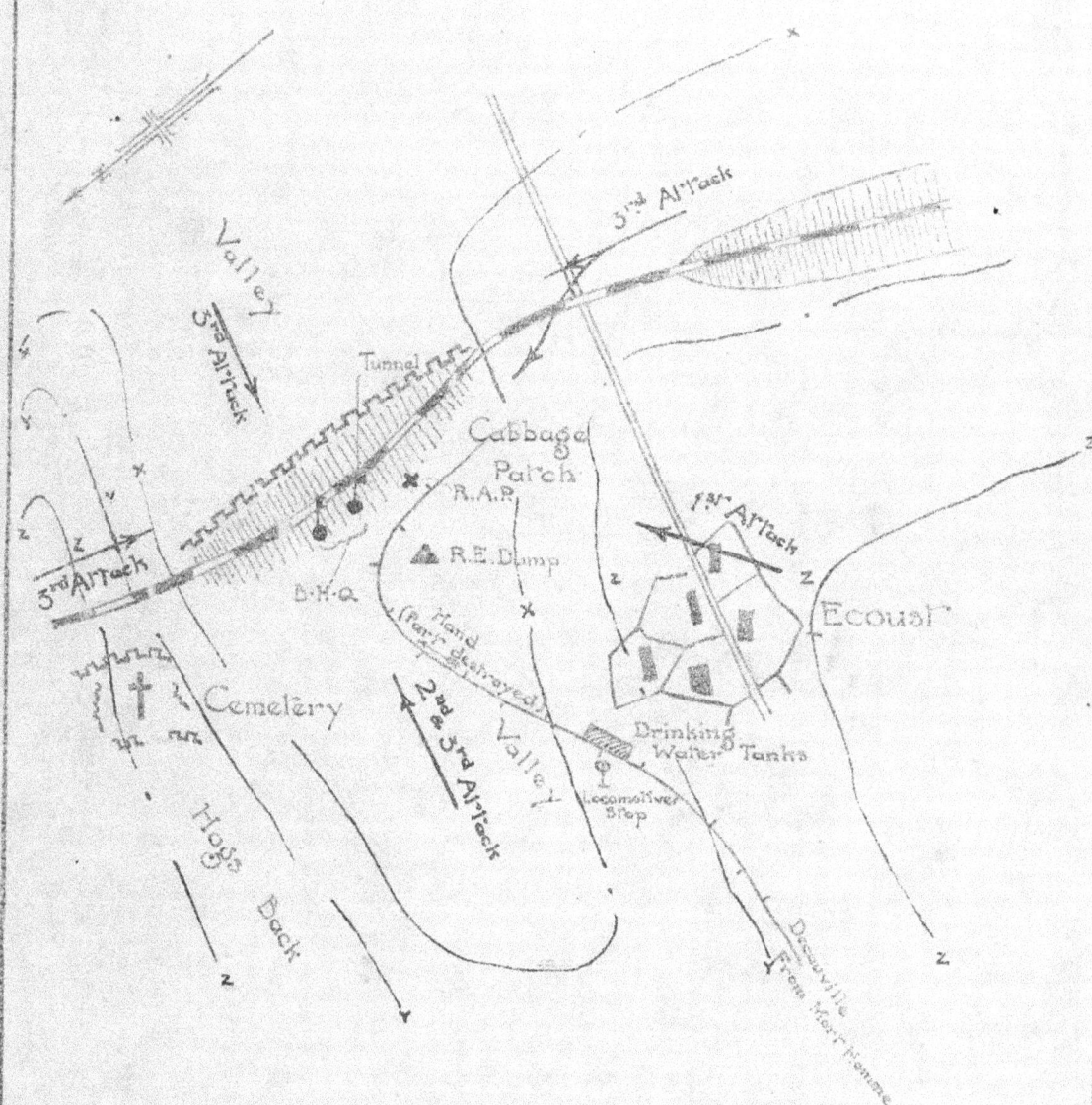

Narrative of the German attack against the 2/6th
Battalion, Sherwood Foresters, on 21st
March, 1918.

The battalion went into the Line on the 9th March. From the first all ranks were acquainted with the fact that the Germans contemplated an offensive and that the battalion front was certain to be attacked if they carried it out, consequently everything possible was done to make the sector strong in defence ... I state this to show that there was no question of surprise.

The 7th Battalion Sherwood Foresters, the right battalion of the Division, linked up with the left battalion of the 6th Division, and the 2/6th Sherwood Foresters continued the line northwards, joining the right battalion of the 176th Brigade just south of BULLECOURT village.

The battalion was organised in depth: two companies in front of the RAILWAY RESERVE - holding advanced posts and the support line: two companies and battalion headquarters in RAILWAY RESERVE.

During the night 20/21st March my patrols were very vigilant, but they failed to notice anything unusual in No Man's Land. (After my capture, a German told me that the attacking troops were lying out in front of the trenches, having taken up their positions earlier in the night.

At 5 a.m. the enemy opened a terrific bombardment with guns of all calibres on to RAILWAY RESERVE, and the same time commenced shelling the posts in front of that line with trench mortars. The bombardment was continuous until 9 a.m. - except for a slight lull at 7 a.m. During the lull I was able to get touch with my posts. I found that the battalion had had few casualties and the situation was well in hand. I informed the brigade of the state of affairs. The bombardment commenced more intensely than ever and continued until 9 a.m. Simultaneously with the artillery lifting, the enemy infantry came forward. This attack was easily stopped, and the enemy was driven back to his own trenches.

For some time things were very quiet and I was able to make reconnaissance, and I found the situation at 9.45 a.m. as follows ... Three of my front posts were holding out; the supports on the left formed a protective flank from TANK AVENUE, but the supporting posts in the rear of the right company had apparently been knocked out by trench mortars fired from the apex. A considerable force of infantry was advancing in that direction and they appeared to have taken all the posts of the battalion on my right. About this time a number of stragglers from the 7th battalion came to my headquarters; these I collected and placed in my trenches. They informed me that the Germans had already taken their own battalion headquarters, and that their battalion was "done in". I was then isolated from the rear, and the enemy was working round my right. I reinforced my right, and as the men went along I explained the situation and told them to do their duty and hold on to the RAILWAY RESERVE at all costs as we were certain to be relieved when our counter-attack was made itself felt. At 10 a.m. my left company in RAILWAY RESERVE reported that the enemy was attacking in strong force from the direction of TANK AVENUE. I was able to reinforce this part of the line, where some extremely bitter fighting took place at close quarters. I was not able to communicate with this company after this, but we could see them holding on and fighting with bombs for some time. At 10.30 a.m. a force of the enemy moved round my flank and occupied SIDNEY AVENUE ... the whole of the RAILWAY EMBANKMENT was at this time enfiladed from the south by trench mortars and machine guns .. I was suffering very heavy losses and it was not possible to collect men to make a bayonet charge which I had ordered to be made.

-1-

The enemy after this bombing, eventually captured the trenches on the embankment up to the Regimental Aid Posts. He had also penetrated on my left. After collecting signallers, runners and servants, battalion headquarters fought (with practically no cover from the rear) until the ammunition was spent, and most of the officers and men were casualties. It was not until we were entirely surrounded that that part of the RAILWAY EMBANKMENT near Battalion Headquarters was taken by the enemy.

I am proud to state that all ranks fought splendidly, and it is difficult, where all did so well, to single out any individuals for special praise, but I should like to bring to your notice the names of the following officers and N.C.Os:-

Captain S.A.Rogers, who commanded the left company in RAILWAY RESERVE, was killed after refusing to surrender. He led his company with great ability, and his personal example was magnificent.

Major A.C.Clarke, although wounded, worked a Lewis gun with much effect and on one occasion used it against a party of enemy who were forming up for attack and inflicted many casualties upon them. He did splendidly all through.

Sec.Lieut. D.St.Leger (R.F.A.) died of wounds the following day. This officer, after the lines of his battery had gone, used a rifle until he was so badly wounded that he was unable to stand. St.Leger was several times wounded, and even when his jaw had been shattered, remained cheerful. He was a real hero.

Sec.Lieut. H.Hickman, A/Adjutant, did well throughout the action and his work collecting stragglers was of great value. He personally destroyed all the correspondence and telephone-apparatus, so that nothing of importance fell into the hands of the enemy.

Sergt.Major - Holroyd set a fine example to us all. He voluntarily took up the task of organising ammunition for the last stand, and regardless of personal danger kept up a supply of bandoliers. This N.C.O's devotion to duty was magnificent.

Sergts.Parson and Mitchell were both killed in the discharge of duties for which they had specially volunteered.

Sec.Lieut. S.M.Johnson (being badly wounded), collected reports throughout the action, and his utter disregard of danger kept up the moral of the men. His work was of great importance & he kept going until he became unconscious.

(Sd) H.S.Hodgkin, Lt.Col.
(4th Dragoon Guards)
Commanding 2/6th Sherwood Fors.

178th Brigade.
59th Division.

2/6th BATTALION

NOTTS. & DERBY REGIMENT

APRIL 1918.

WAR DIARY

2/6TH - BN. THE SHERWOOD FORESTERS

APRIL 1918.

WAR DIARY
or
INTELLIGENCE SUMMARY

Army Form C. 2118

Place	Date	Hour	Summary of Events and Information	Remarks and references to Appendices
Sheets 27 + 28			Fighting Strength 18 Offs + 364 O.R's.	
CAMBLIGNEUL	1/4/18		Proceeded to AUBIGNY by March route, there entrained for PROVEN. Marched from PROVEN to Road Camp.	
	2/7/4/18		Road Camp. 7.25 b.i.4. Arrived at 10 a.m 2/4/18.	
WINNEZEELE	8/4/18	10 a.m	Marched to WINNEZEELE. Arrived at 2.0 p.m.	
	10/4/18	2 p.m	Entrained at WINNEZEELE and proceeded to POPERINGHE. Marched to Tent camp, BRANDHOEK. Arrived 7.0 p.m. In VIII Corps Reserve.	
BRANDHOEK	11/4/18		C.O. reconnoitred the area DICKEBUSCH and VIERSTRAAT with the idea of reinforcing. A Dismounted personnel entrained at BRANDHOEK at 3.0 p.m and detrained at LA CLYTTE. Transport moved by road to DRANOUTRE area. Battn. ordered to move up the KEMMEL - LA CLYTTE road where it halted and billeted in barns near road.	
	12/4/18	10 p.m	Battn moved up KEMMEL - NEUVE EGLISE road as enemy were reported to have broken through and moving Northwards.	
		12 m.n.	Situation normal, as Battn ordered to Camp in KEMMEL - CHATEAU wood. Patrol sent down road to confirm situation, they reach NEUVE EGLISE without opposition.	
	13/4/18		During the afternoon Battn. took up Line N.27.c.0.5 to N.28.d.0.4. Battn. ordered to move up and take over the dispositions of the 7th Bn. S.J. in Valley of DOUVE in Brigade Reserve, and be ready to counter attack NEUVE EGLISE should enemy capture village. Move commenced at M.N. 13/14th and completed.	
	14/4/18		Orders received to send out patrols to get in touch with 71st Inf Bde. on line N.19.b by T1 and T2. Touch gained before daylight. Heavily shelled throughout the day.	

WAR DIARY
or
INTELLIGENCE SUMMARY.
(Erase heading not required.)

Army Form C. 2118.

Place	Date	Hour	Summary of Events and Information	Remarks and references to Appendices
	14/4/18		About midday orders received to fill gap on the road in T.9.d.	
		11 p.m	About 11.0 p.m orders received to withdraw to main line of Resistance, i.e. Railway line running through T.1.c and T.2.b and d, T.3 Central, along the ridge T6 Central, T.5 Central to T.6 Central. Battn Hd.Qrs established at N.26.b.6.1.	
	15/4/18		Orders received about 11.0 pm to withdraw to the KEMMEL-METEREN Line. Battn took up outpost position in front of KEMMEL. Defences from N.23.c.3.8. to N.27.c.7.4.	
	16/4/18	2.45 am	Withdrawal took place about 2.0 am Outposts left out until the effect that the 28th French Division would attack at 6.0 p.m in between WULVERGHEM and WYTSCHAETE with their right flank resting on the LINDENHOEK- WULVERGHEM road. Battn ordered to advance with leading wave and establish a defensive flank on line N.32.d.2.3 – N.33.c.9.1. and N.33.b.5.0. This attack did not take place.	
	17/4/18		About 10.0 am enemy commenced heavy bombardment and attacked all along the line. Attack held up but gap was covered on left of Batn front. This gap was filled by one Coy of 2/5th Bn. S.Y's. During the evening a party of the enemy advanced to within 100 yds of our line and on being fired on retired with the exception of an Officer who remained sniping	

Army Form C. 2118.

WAR DIARY
or
INTELLIGENCE SUMMARY.
(Erase heading not required.)

Instructions regarding War Diaries and Intelligence Summaries are contained in F.S. Regs., Part II. and the Staff Manual respectively. Title pages will be prepared in manuscript.

Place	Date	Hour	Summary of Events and Information	Remarks and references to Appendices
	18/4/18		2 Lt W. Jackson went out and captured the Officer single handed in broad daylight.	
		About 1.0 p.m	the trench was visited on having Aircraft "Jam" bombarded. The Battn. therefore had to withdraw. The bombardment did not take place and the Battn. returned	
		about 4.0 p.m		
	19/4/18		The Battn. was relieved by the French leaving the line at 4.30 a.m. Proceeded to Billets at WESTHOUTRE.	
		1.0 p.m	Moved by rail to BRAKE CAMP, A.30 Central.	
	20/4/18	12 noon	Marched to HOUTKERQUE, E.20.d.25.75.	
HOUTKERQUE	26/4/18		Battn. digging on WATOU-CAESTRE Line.	
F 25 b.1.4.	27/4/18 28/4/18		Marched to ROAD CAMP, F.25.b.1.4. Bn training carried out.	
HOUTKERQUE	29/4/18 30/4/18		Marched to HOUTKERQUE, E.20.d.25.75.	
			Fighting Strength 31 Offrs. 836. O.R.s.	

W.B. Capt. & Adjt.
2/6th Bn Sherwood Foresters.

SECRET

WARNING ORDER
71st Infantry Brigade.

31/7/18.

1.   The 71st Infantry Brigade will relieve the 18th Infantry Brigade in the Left Sector of the Divisional front on 2nd/3rd August 1918.

2.   The 9th Norfolk Regt. will relieve the right front Battn.
        The 2nd Sherwood Foresters will relieve the left front Bn.
        The 1st Leicestershire Regt. will be in reserve.

3.   A Battalion of the 27th American Division will be attached to the 71st Infantry Brigade for 8 days commencing the same evening. Sections and Platoons of this Battalion will join the Companies of the British Battalions to which they are being attached, before the 71st Infantry Brigade moves up to take over the line.

4.   Detailed instructions regarding the above attachment will be issued later.

5.   Acknowledge.

                                                        Captain,
            A/Brigade Major, 71st Infantry Brigade.

Copy to   Lieut. Col. Commdg.
            Brigade Major,
            Staff Captain,
            Signalling Officer,
            B. T. O.
            B. I. O.
            Norfolk Regt.
            Leicestershire Regt.
            Sherwood Foresters.
            T.M. Battery.

SECRET

Reference 71st Infantry Brigade Warning Order issued to-day.

1. Dispositions of 18th Infantry Brigade are as follows :-

1st K.S.L.I.	In Reserve,	Hqtrs at H.26.d.30.30.
2nd Y. & L.	Right Front,	Hqtrs at H.28.a.20.00.
1st The Buffs.	Left Front,	Hqtrs at H.26.d.30.00.
18th T.M. Battery.		Hqtrs at H.26.d.30.30.

Reconnaissances should be made as early as possible.

2. Usual forward parties will be sent forward tomorrow night to live with their opposite numbers until relief takes place.

31/7/1918.   A/Brigade Major, 71st Infantry Brigade.
Captain,

To all recipients of 71st Inf. Bde. W.O.

4.45 a:m should read 4.45
p:m — see diary —

[signature]

3/11/30.

Line 5 from the bottom "Left" should apparently read "right"

29/10/30

Vol/16

WAR DIARY

2/6 Bn The Sherwood Foresters.

MAY 1918.

ORIGINAL

15.W.

Army Form C. 2118.

WAR DIARY
or
INTELLIGENCE SUMMARY.
(Erase heading not required.)

Instructions regarding War Diaries and Intelligence Summaries are contained in F. S. Regs., Part II. and the Staff Manual respectively. Title pages will be prepared in manuscript.

Place	Date	Hour	Summary of Events and Information	Remarks and references to Appendices
Sheet 27.			Fighting Strength 31 Offrs. 836 O.R.s	
HOUTKERQUE E.20.b.25.75	1.5.18		Battalion training carried out.	
	2.5.18	5.15pm	Battalion moved by March route to bivouac at K.17.a.3.3 (NT WATOU)	
K.17.a.3.3	3.5.18		Battalion employed as a Digging Party on WATOU–CASTRE front	
	4.5.18	5.20pm	Reserve Lines	
	5.5.18	9.0am	Battalion entrained at E.28.d.6.6. and proceeded to Barracks, ST OMER.	
HAZEBROUCK 5A				
ST OMER	6.5.18			
	7.5.18		16 Offrs & 665 O.R.s transferred to 16 Inf Base Depot CALAIS, and remainder of Battalion formed into Batt Training to be Establishment 10 Offrs 4th O.R.s.	
BLESSY 53.d.95.40.	9.5.18	8.0am	Training Cadre marched to BLESSY.	
SHEET 13b	10.5.18	8.0am	Training Cadre marched to BOURS.	
BOURS H.34.b.9.7	11.5.18		Training of Staff carried out.	
	31.5.18			

Capt. & Adjt.
O.C. 2/8th Bn. The Sherwood Foresters

CONFIDENTIAL

WAR DIARY

OF

HQ 2/6 Sherwood Foresters
(TRAINING CADRE)

FOR

JUNE 1918.

ORIGINAL.

WAR DIARY
2/6th Bn The Sherwood Foresters
JUNE 1918.

TO:-   Headquarters,
              178th. Infantry Brigade.

         Herewith Original Copy of WAR DIARY for
the Month of JUNE 1918.

                                    Lieut.Col.,
1st. July 1918.   Comdg. 2/6th. Bn. The Sherwood Foresters.

WAR DIARY
INTELLIGENCE SUMMARY. June 1918.

(Erase heading not required.)

Army Form C. 2118.

Place	Date	Hour	Summary of Events and Information	Remarks and references to Appendices
BOURS. H.34.b.9.7. (44 B)	1.6.18		Fighting Strength :- Officers --- 10 O.R.'s --- 43	
	1.6.18 to 16.6.18		Training of Staff carried out.	
	17.6.18	6.0 a.m.	Moved by March route to FONTAINE-lez-BOULANE.	
FONTAINE-lez-BOULANE. F.29.d.8.8. (44c Eastern Half)	18.6.18 to 30.6.18		Part of Staff assisting at 59th Divisional School - remainder assisting in training 13th Bn (G) West Riding Regt.	
	30.6.18		Fighting Strength:- Officers --- 10 O.R.'s --- 43	

D Mican
Lieut: Col.
C/O. 29th Bn. The Sherwood Foresters.

95
2/6th Bn. THE SHERWOOD FORESTERS. (Training Cadre) 95/18

WAR DIARY.

JULY 1918.

17.W.

Army Form C. 2118.

WAR DIARY
or
INTELLIGENCE SUMMARY.
(Erase heading not required.)

July 1918

Place	Date	Hour	Summary of Events and Information	Remarks and references to Appendices
			Fighting Strength. Officers 10 O.R. 143	
FONTAINE LES BOULANS	9/7/18		Notification received that the 2/8th Bn. Sherwood Foresters Training Cadre be disbanded and the personnel placed at the disposal of the G.O.C. 59th Division for posting within that Division (Authority - First Army's No. 6835/25a, under 6/7/18 & 59th Divn No. A1830/30/24 dated July 9th 1918).	AP
H.Q. etc & Skeleton Cadre n/am				AP
	28/7/18	11 a.m.	Left FONTAINE LES BOULANS and proceeded by motor bus to BARLY (1P.15.a. 08.) Billeted in Chateau	AP
BARLY (P.15.a. 08) (Sheet 57.E.)	28/7/18 30/7/18 31/7/18		Portion of the Draining Cadre posted to units within 59th Division. Thirteen unduring officers Wot Yorks, & M.C. proceed to Bord. Etaples as per personal Instruction No/330.30/24 Remainder of the Training Cadre posted to units within 59th Division.	AP
	1/7/18 to 31/7/18		Portion of the Draining Cadre instructing at 59th Divl School according to the training of the 1/3 Bh. West Riding Regt. Remainder	AP
	31/7/18		Fighting Strength :- Nil	AP

A.P. Duma, Capt. & Adjt.,
2/8th Bn. The Sherwood Foresters.

www.ingramcontent.com/pod-product-compliance
Lightning Source LLC
Chambersburg PA
CBHW051527190426
43193CB00045BA/2371